Girl, Get Up and Move!

Going To Your Next Level

Rynette Upson-Bush

RELENTLESS
PUBLISHING

Co-Authors

Marc Betancourt
Bridgette Burks
Janell Chambers
Aisha Chamorro
Auguste Crenshaw
Carole Davis
LaToya Frazier
Andrea Green
Gwen Green
Cynthia Jackson
Kijafa James
DeShonda Jennings
Taynia Mosley
Eboni Montsho
Maude Nelson
Amber Nicole
Baruti Akiiki Abdallah-Nosakhere
Dr. Sonya Poitier
Nasonya Rowell
Joshua Smith
Rynette Upson-Bush
LisaBeth Willis
Jacqueline Wilson

Get Up Girl and Move ! : Going To Your Next Level
Copyright © 2020 by Rynette Upson-Bush.

Published by :
Relentless Publishing House
www.relentlesspublishing.com

ISBN: 978-1-948829-67-0

Table of Contents

Introduction

Throughout my life I struggled with low self esteem, no self worth, self limiting beliefs, and I dwelled in negativity everyday. Even though I went to church and believed in God I didn't believe in me. It wasn't until I got around the right group of people that my life changed. No matter where you come from, no matter what you have been through you have to make a difference in your own life.

The ball is in your court. How you play the game will ultimately make the difference of how your story ends. You can continue to lay down and whine, complain, and sit in a pity party or you can choose to get up and move! I'm so glad I got up and chose to move instead of laying down and accepting what life gave me. I have learned that I must create my own reality and you can do the same!

I lost my six-year-old grandson, Sean Michael Bridges, in a tragic car accident in the process of trying to do this project but because I know that God called me to make a difference. Through His strength, I drew strength. I knew I had to get up and move. God is a healer, deliverer and everything you need. Trust him in all that you do. Life is going to happen but it's our response that makes the difference. Your story can be different when you choose to get up and make a difference.

This is an inspirational tool of motivation, transformation, stories of triumph and action steps to help you and women all over the world to get up and go create the reality they want to see. If you're reading this book it's obvious you're looking for more. It's your time and your turn. Enjoy this book, hear the messages, do the work, and get up and move! This book was written to help you and women.

Blessings

Rynette Upson-Bush

Girl, You got this. Now it's time to go get it!

Get Up!

Then Jesus said to him, "Get up! Pick up your mat and walk."

John 5:8

I'm so excited that you have chosen to invest in this book! This is an inspirational tool designed to ignite you and excite you to get up and go after what God said you can have. Many times, we are the ones holding ourselves from our destiny. Yes, I know what you're going to say, "he did this", "she did that", "the boss was unfair", "I was betrayed." I want you to understand I know it hurts. I know it's a hard pill to swallow and I'm not making light of it. I've been in that place too, trying to get through the trials and tribulations of life. However, it is our response to situations that truly keep us stuck and limited. Even if what happened wasn't your fault, it is your fault when you choose to stay stuck in a situation that you have the power to change.

This man who was sitting at the pool of Bethesda sat there for many years holding on to this mat. He treasured this mat more than he treasured God. He was holding on to his mat as if his life depended on it. It was a prized possession in his eyes. He slept on it, sat on it, clung to it as if it was attached to him. He sat on that mat and watched the world pass him by. He was so attached to that mat he couldn't imagine living without it so when Jesus told him to pick it up and walk, he didn't do it. He made every excuse to remain on the mat. He told Jesus he couldn't get up and walk. He didn't have the faith to move. He preferred to make excuses. We can make excuses like the man in this scripture or we can get up and move and make things happen!

What has God told you to do that you aren't doing? What mat are you holding on to? What excuses are you making that are holding you back from God's best? Just like the man at the pool of Bethesda, Girl it's time to pick up your mat and move. When Jesus was finished with the man at the pool, he didn't need the mat anymore. Listen to me and listen real good. No amount of money, no man, no relationship, no career or materialistic things can do what God can do! No amount of worry, anxiety, fear or anything else is greater than God. It's time to trust God and allow Him to carry it all because He can. What's too much for us is nothing for God. God has a hope and a great planned future for you. Are you ready to pick up your mat and walk? Your biggest dreams, visions, and all that you want is waiting for you. The key is you must listen to His command and walk. Girl it's time to get up and move!!

This book is compiled with stories of triumph, hope, positive affirmations, inspirational messages, and action steps to inspire you to get up and move!! It's your time and turn to pick up your mat and walk!! Let's GO!

Rynette Upson-Bush

What excuses do yu need to let go of and move on from?

_____

_____

_____

_____

_____

_____

_____

_____

What has God told you to do that you aren't doing?

_____

_____

_____

_____

_____

_____

_____

NOTES

THROUGH THE FIRE

She is clothed with strength, dignity and she laughs without fear of the future.

Proverbs 31:25

This verse is so powerful. It has been the driving force behind why I continue to persevere every day, even when I don't feel like it and trust me there has been plenty of those days. But before I get into that, let me introduce myself. My name is Amber Nicole and I am a Confidence Coach.

My God given purpose is to inspire women that struggle with past trauma, life issues and who are looking for a change. I coach, empower and help women develop the confidence needed to achieve their specific goals throughout our sessions. I've been where you are, my life has never been easy. I was molested at eleven years old and pregnant at twelve by the same man. I used to live in low income housing growing up with roaches and mice. I was in a relationship with an abusive man for a decade. These are some of the hardships I've endured with fortitude so hear me and feel me when I say, I have been through the fire many times.

But here I stand, fiercely overcoming all hurdles of life. Growing up, I wished my mother would have told me "although you will go through a lot of hardships in your life, never allow that to break you and always love yourself first". Those simple words along with her

9

guidance and protection would have probably saved me from severe depression, lack of confidence and my broken mindset.

After countless failures, I had to tell myself "Girl Get Up and Move!" The question asked is how do you begin to elevate with no real guidance? Do you realize how powerful your mind is? In order to level up, you must be intentional about the thoughts you think. Our thoughts dictate our actions! The quote that continues to help me is "If you realize the power of your thoughts, you'd never think a negative thought again". Your mind is your most powerful resource which, is why the enemy is always after it. Don't let him win. Fear and lack of resources is the major reason why people don't succeed in life. What if I said, "it's all in your mind?" The truth is the only obstacle in your way is you. You must believe you are limitless! Every morning, before I start my business, "Justyce" By Amber Nicole, I pray for all the things that are good in my life. I don't focus on what I'm lacking, but I show gratitude for all that I have. My good health, a roof over my head, my children, food to eat, and other simple things we take for granted. Daily prayer, meditation, visualizing, and the Law of Attraction helps me stay focused on my purpose. Queens, collectively this is the game changer.

Amber Nicole

How can you prepare your mind to elevate and move past your obstacles?

_____

_____

_____

_____

_____

_____

_____

_____

What is the "WHY" to keep you pushing forward?

_____

_____

_____

_____

_____

_____

_____

_____

NOTES

UNNOTICED

Pardon me, my lord, Gideon replied, but if the LORD is with us, why has all this happened to us? Where are all his wonders that our ancestors told us about...

Judges 6:13

Has there ever been a time you've felt unnoticed by people or even God? Let that sink in for a moment. Things, situations, and circumstances can line up so perfectly to convince you of such. Not only does it feel like nobody sees you, but you can become so engulfed by the shouting lies of the enemy that it can feel as though not even God cares or notices you. Such a time recently gripped me and latched its tentacles into my mind, repeatedly pumping its poison into my bloodstreams. Shortly after, I participated in a service where people were receiving divine visitation, a personal prophetic word, and special attention all around me except for ME!

Outwardly, I wore the appearance that all was good, but inwardly, I was tumbling headfirst into a pit of despair, anger, and unworthiness. I was so overcome by the moment that everything unified itself against me like an unyielding bully. Reminding me that somehow down this journey called life, I hadn't measured up enough for God to see me. I mean really see me. I absolutely hated it. This makes me think about the story of Gideon in Judges 6:13 He, like me, felt unnoticed by God. Everything around him convinced him that he wasn't good enough. In Gideon's mind, their clan was the weakest in Manasseh, and he believed he was the least likely in his father's house. I mean he and his people were being mercilessly oppressed by their enemy for seven years. So when the Angel of the Lord said to him, "The Lord is with you, mighty warrior!" Gideon was not easily convinced. But God, being the loving Father that He is, wouldn't just let up without a fight. Later in the chapter, God took the time to re-convince Gideon of the truth He knew about him. I, too, needed re-convincing, that God was for me and not against me. That He loved me and nothing ever made Him stop loving me, and most importantly, that he noticed ME.

What an illuminatingly freeing truth. Romans 8:38-39 leaves no room for doubt of this. God came after me and rescued me from the tentacles I mentioned earlier. It wasn't an easy win. God surrounded me with loving believers of Christ who literally stood beside me, pushed me, and prayed me out of that bottomless pit. Thank you, Jesus! He noticed where I was and came after me using those loving jewels of the Faith. He IS FOR ME and not against me. I challenge you to look the enemy of your soul in the eye and reject his lies with TRUTH that is available in the word of God. And don't be afraid to receive help through prayer along the way. "You Are Enough!"

Maude´ Nelson

Think about where you are today within yourself. What are you believing about YOU today?

_____

_____

_____

_____

_____

_____

_____

_____

What are those stolen truths?

_____

_____

_____

_____

_____

_____

_____

_____

NOTES

THROUGH IT ALL

Trust in the LORD with all thine heart; and lean not unto thine own understanding. In all thy ways acknowledge him, and he shall direct thy paths.

Proverbs 3:5-6

As the New Year of 2007 came in I was beyond excited because I was about to do what most people wouldn't accomplish in a lifetime. I did what only 37% of households do...I paid off my house. After losing my last house to foreclosure, it was a blessing to be able to pay off a home. I was so excited, no more mortgage for me! This was shaping up to be one of the best years in my life. Then one day what seemed to be the best year of my life turned out to be one of the most horrific years in my entire life. On August 31, 2007, my third heartbeat and youngest son was brutally murdered. Willie was only 22 years old at the time of his demise. That day I felt like my entire world was shattered in an instant. There was the biggest hole and excruciating pain in my heart. I had no clue of how to even begin to piece my life back together after such a tragic loss.

While grieving the loss of my youngest son there was a void in my heart that seemed like a world of darkness and total despair. This was too much for me, but I knew it wasn't too much for God. The section of the scripture "lean not to your own understanding" stuck with me as I fought to deal with his death. I never got over my son's passing, but I got through with continued prayer. I fought hard not to allow his deaths to get the best of me.

I wasn't sure if I could take another person, I loved dying. On February 9, 2019, I received an emergency call to get to the hospital; only to find out my dear mother passed away. I was totally devastated. I had to figure out how I was going to keep moving forward, because I was so close to graduating, returning to school after 30 years to get my college degree. Through God I continued to press and on June 2019 I was slated to graduate with my Arts of Science in Human Resources.

My pastor had proclaimed the year of 2019 as the new wine season, "Expect the Unexpected" was the theme. I didn't know at the beginning of 2019 how significant this would be in my life. I had to deal with the unexpected in 2019, but God is so faithful. Through all of the tragedies and pain, I discovered I had staying power and the strength to move mountains. Most people wouldn't have survived such a heart wrenching, gut punching year like the one I had, but through it all I made it. I continued to go to school and graduated with my degree June 29, 2019.

To God be the glory it was His strength and His grace that I made it! I share my story to let the world know that you can get up and move on and not just survive through the tough times, but you can thrive when you keep God first. Girl get up and move and let God carry you through..

God's will...God's way...God's Timing

Cynthia Jackson

What unexpected event or circumstances do you need to get up from?

_____

_____

_____

_____

_____

_____

_____

_____

How can you come out triumphant through your trials?

_____

_____

_____

_____

_____

_____

_____

_____

NOTES

STRENGTH FOR IT

I can do all things through Christ who strengthens me

Philippians 4:13

Life is full of many challenges that we all face. It's how we handle those challenges that will help us get through! I've faced many obstacles throughout my life and I have refused to allow them to defeat me. I want to share with you one obstacle that has changed my life. Three years ago, I was diagnosed with Lupus. Sitting with my doctor, as he read the results, all I could say to myself was "What? No! How could this be?" My world instantly came crashing down. I felt as though I was the star of my own movie with no escape. My body began to feel numb and I felt empty inside. I didn't want to believe this. I had so many questions that needed to be answered.

So, I gave myself permission to cry for an hour and put myself together before breaking the news to my family. I looked at it this way, I had two options: Fight this battle OR be defeated! I was not about to give up and be defeated. That was not an option.

God has given me this unbelievable strength to continue to fight this battle with Lupus and to keep pushing on despite the odds against me. Everyday my body is in pain, the pain is so bad at times where I just don't want to move, but I always find the strength to push through each day, work, and taking care of my family. You see, I realized I had to be shaken up to be reminded of my purpose. God has a plan for me and I intend to live my life to the fullest! Life is delicate and most of us don't realize how precious it is until it's too late. We never know the battles that people are fighting. But always remember, you can rise against any situation and achieve your dreams.

What is holding you back from becoming a better you? What has to happen to you in order to for you to live your life to your fullest potential? Start where you are. Start with fear. Start with pain. Start with doubt. Start with hands shaking. Start with voice trembling, but start. Start and DON'T STOP! Start where you are with what you have…just start. You can do it!

Living with Lupus has been a difficult journey, but I remain resilient. I refuse to let a five-letter word change or stop me. In life, you may not have a choice on what obstacles come your way, but you do have a choice on how you deal with and overcome them. Do not let a moment in life define or defeat you because you, my friend, are unstoppable.

Aisha Chamorro

What is shaking your strength?

_____

_____

_____

_____

_____

_____

_____

_____

How will you combat it and remain strong?

_____

_____

_____

_____

_____

_____

_____

_____

NOTES

PERFECTLY IMPERFECT

I will lift up my eyes to the hills-from whence comes my help? My help comes from the Lord, who made heaven and earth.

Psalms 121:12

Life happens. We've heard this cliché over and over again, and yet it's never easy to adjust. We're told that 'all things work together for the good to those who love the Lord,' but when we've experienced a level of personal hell, it's never easy to embrace the challenge and just "be still." Why is it that life has to be so difficult at times even though we try to do the right things, and have chosen Christ as our savior whom we depend upon? Well, I won't even pretend to know the answer to that question, however, I do know that God allows us to experience challenges and we must be reliant on Him and determined to win, if we want to come out on top.

There was a time when I thought I had life figured out and my path was clear. Then God presented me with a choice. I later discovered it was actually a test. One path was a walk of faith that would lead to entrepreneurship and the other was a return to the comfort of the corporate world. Working in corporate is predictable; to me it was familiar as I had worked in my industry for almost twenty years, and I enjoyed it immensely.

Historically, I am not much of a risk taker, so I accepted the job and immediately there was a price to pay; in fact, at times it seemed as though more went wrong than right. Among other issues, I had a work injury that caused me to be on short term disability leave for almost five months. On the outside, I looked and sounded the same, only my family and a few close friends knew the depth of my suffering. I set project goals, only to watch the dates of completion pass me by with the best of intention. My confidence waned as I doubted whether or not my full capacity would be restored. What a way to start a job!

In the midst of it all, I remained perfectly imperfect. Seeking God, while yet trying to figure things out on my own, the very human thing to do. Over time, with cognitive and physical therapy, as well as meditation, I began to feel normal again.

Even now as I fight to get back to pre-injury weight, I sometimes have moments where I have to pause and refocus because the load feels too heavy. It is then when I call out to God for His strength to carry me.

Perhaps you are faced with a test or struggling with a major decision. How will you pass the test? Will you have the courage to do things God's way or your own? Whatever the case, know that God will be with you, and if you fall, forgive yourself and get back up again.

Girl, your outcome is different. You have the victory.

LisaBeth Willis

What tests are you currently going through?

_____

_____

_____

_____

_____

_____

_____

_____

What steps will you take to pass the tests?

_____

_____

_____

_____

_____

_____

_____

_____

NOTES

HEALING FOR YOUR FUTURE

Therefore, if anyone is in Christ, the new creation has come: The old has gone, the new is here!

2 Corinthians 5:17

I love this scripture because it speaks so powerfully to my life. For years, I desired a change in my life because I didn't like the direction my life was heading. My relationship with God had to change for me to move forward. God changed me, and that changed my heart and who I was as a person. I love the fact that you don't have to stay stuck in who people think you are. If you are a person filled with compromise and insecurities God is so forgiving that His grace continues to forgive no matter how many times we mess up. He gives us a chance to change into who He called us to be. The Bible is filled with people that God changed and used for His glory: Jacob was a con artist, who became a righteous man. Rahab was a prostitute who later became a part of the lineage of Jesus. Each day is an opportunity to decide to start again and rise to a new level or stay in mediocrity and compromise.

Too often, people sit back and wish for things to be different in their lives; like it will just magically appear, but it won't. You must put in the work to see the things you want manifested in your life. I've found out that many people look at me and think I've lived some type of charmed life, but that's far from the truth. The truth is that I decided that I no longer wanted to be stuck in mediocrity and lack. I wanted to heal from my painful past and have a life I am passionate about. I believed that it was possible, so I started to pray, dream, and hope for a better life. Then I started to step out of my comfort zone to get the life I always dreamed of. As I stepped out, I realized that I had to set goals, make plans and do the work towards the goals to see them manifest. I started this journey with allowing God to heal my heart and emotions from all the unhealthy, toxic relationships from my past. I set standards and boundaries for the new people that I allowed into my life. I worked hard to think about what I wanted in my life and what I needed to do to create that life. As I started my new walk with God and healing journey to live a life of my dreams many doors closed, but I've learned every door that opens isn't for me.

Now when a door closes, I don't let it devastate me. I know that God has something better for me and I work towards opening a new door. I don't allow people's rejection or personal choices wound me anymore; that's where loving yourself comes in. Now, I move towards the people who appreciate and value me and release those who don't. You have to invest in yourself to obtain the things that you want in life. Nobody is going to just give it to you. The work you put in won't be easy. You have to believe in and support yourself when no one else does. You may have to pursue some counseling, training or mentoring. By any means necessary do what it takes and follow your dreams.

There is hard work and sacrifice that comes with obtaining dreams, but with hard work, you can step out and rise up to a new beginning in your life. Healing is a journey. It's liberating to step out and overcome all obstacles and move in the directions of your dreams. Girl get up you can do this!

Nasonya Rowell

Who and what do you need to let go of in order to truly heal?

_____

_____

_____

_____

_____

_____

_____

_____

How will your life look when you complete your healing journey?

_____

_____

_____

_____

_____

_____

_____

NOTES

FEARFULLY AND WONDERFULLY MADE

I will praise thee: for I am fearfully and wonderfully made: marvelous are thy works: and that my soul knoweth right well.

Psalm 139:14

How many times have you listened to someone else tell you negative things about yourself? What often happens when women begin to lose themselves is that they begin to listen to someone else's assessment of who they are. We have to learn that the only opinion of us that matters is God's always forgiving acceptance and love. It is so easy to lose sight of that if every day someone is allowed to speak to you in a disparaging way. We all have made choices in life of which we are not proud. We are often our own worst critics. Somehow, we must come to a place of acceptance. We are important to and loved by our Creator. We must learn to allow that fact to resonate inside us every day!

Gwen Russell Green

What do you do with your time that consistently makes you feel better when you have done it?

_____

_____

_____

_____

_____

_____

_____

_____

Who can you consistently reach out to and receive positive support?

_____

_____

_____

_____

_____

_____

_____

_____

NOTES

Girl believe anything is possible because it is.

I'D RATHER SACRIFICE THAN SETTLE

Why do you spend your money for that which is not bread and you labor for that which does not satisfy? Listen diligently to me and eat what is good and delight yourself in rich food.

Isiah 55:2

Have you given up on thinking you can get the good stuff and are settling for the inferior? Are you living your life to the fullest or are you just existing? Life is meant to live and not just exist. If you are doing anything other than living you are existing and settling. God is our father and we are His children. Yes, the apple of His eye and the object of His affection. Do you think He really wants us settling? God is ready to give us the desires of our heart, but we must be ready to receive all He has for us.

How many times will you continue to say, "I hate my job", "I'm sick of being treated like this", "I hate this neighborhood", "I know I should be doing something different", "I know there is more?" The list can go on. Are you guilty of doing this? Well, if you are settling in any area of your life it's time you decide to get up and change that story!

It's the many lies and excuses that you've told yourself so that you could settle comfortably and not feel bad that you have allowed yourself to sit in mediocrity, scarcity, lack, limited thinking, unsatisfied and unfulfilled. When you choose not to live up to your fullest potential and live out your God given purpose you will never live the life you were meant to live. Do you know you deserve better than how you've been living?

You know you want more but you've settled or let people make you feel you're wrong for wanting more. You apologize and downplay your success to make others feel good. If they didn't step up to the plate and do what they needed to do that is not your issue. Let them keep their problems and issues and make a decision to not settle when you know you want and deserve more. Girl it's time to get up and move and pursue your passion and purpose and live your life the way you want...the way God intended it to be. Own your dreams and be unapologetic about what God said you can have!!

Have faith for what God said is yours and take the necessary steps to accomplish everything you always wanted! Don't be lazy or settle when it comes to your life. Make it count ....um you only get one!! Philippians 3:14 says press towards the mark of the higher calling. Yes, honey you have been called to higher and you know it. Don't ever settle for anything less than the best!

Rynette Upson- Bush

What are you settling for and why?

_____

_____

_____

_____

_____

_____

_____

_____

Do you seriously own your dreams? Why or why not?

_____

_____

_____

_____

_____

_____

_____

_____

NOTES

BE THE LIGHT

Let your light so shine before men, that they may see your good works, and glorify your Father which is in heaven.

Matthew 5:16

One candle can spark the light of every candle in a room. Sharing your light won't ever diminish your glow. In fact, your light will continue to shine brightly even after the flame has been passed to someone else. The possibilities for success, growth and progress are far greater when our combined light illuminates the spaces we occupy.

Light exists in various forms. I love nature and marvel at the intensity and wonder of the sun. The light that radiates from it is so powerful that the entire solar system revolves around it. On a clear sunny day, you can see the beautiful sun rays peeking through the fluffy white clouds in the sky. That image reminds me of the light that God shines on us. Those rays of light help to bring forth new growth and sustain life all over the world. Because I was raised to believe there is enough sun to shine on everyone, I am thankful that we can all bask in the glow of God's love and light.

There will also be days when we may feel our torch doesn't burn as brightly as it should. Remain encouraged and never let distractions or naysayers dim your light. When insecurity creeps in during uncertain times, remember that the spirit of God is always able to reignite us when our flame dwindles to embers. God is the light of the world and His light dwells within us.

Whether it is one person passing light to another or God's amazing light shining on us all. I will be forever grateful for the light that brightens our paths as we go through life's journey. The Lord is my light and my salvation. I have been blessed to be a blessing to others and I realize to whom much is given much is required. I will continue to let my little light shine and give God all the praise and glory while doing so. In loving memory of Dr. Vera Joyce Rose Poitier...the most radiant woman I have ever known.

Daily Declaration
Today I will consciously spread love and light...and I will do the same thing tomorrow and the next day.

"Light is to darkness what love is to fear; in the presence of one the other disappears." –Marianne Williamson

Sonya Poitier

What are some ways we can celebrate the blessing of God's light and share it with others in need?

_____

_____

_____

_____

_____

_____

_____

_____

What self-care measures can you take to keep your glow?

_____

_____

_____

_____

_____

_____

_____

_____

NOTES

A FRESH START

For I know the plans I have for you, declares the Lord, plans to prosper you and not to harm you, plans to give hope and a future.

Jeremiah 29:11

Thank God, He saw fit to allow me to live and tell my story. This is not an experience I would want anyone to to take a journey on. My husband and I were headed home after a long day of work. On this particular day the drive seemed extremely long. Our marriage had been rocky for a while. On today it felt like everything we could argue and scream about we did. I decided I was tired of everything. I couldn't take it anymore. I did not understand why or how my life went wrong. All I knew at that moment, that my life wasn't worth living anymore and I wanted to end it all today.

My mind reflected back to a lady I once knew that ended her life. I never contemplated about taking my own life, but this was the day that leaving this world seemed more like the right thing to do. After 18 years of marriage, I made a decision I never felt I would have to make. I filed for divorce. Divorce wasn't my first choice, but after years of trying to make my marriage work I finally realized that it wasn't meant to be. No one knows all the reasons why marriages fall apart, but sometimes they just does. This was the most painful time in my life. I really thought we were going to make it work. Our children were graduating from high school and starting college. I wanted to work on ourselves, to put our marriage first again. I felt lost, overlooked and desired attention from my husband. Everyday things seemed to get worse and I began sinking into a deep depression and I felt suicide was my only way out. I allowed the situation and my emotions to get the best of me. I didn't know what to do, and I was too afraid to ask for help. I was so unhappy and hurting I set out to take my life. To this day I really can't tell you what happened. I didn't know who I was, where I was, or what even happened to me. After losing consciousness I woke up in a hospital. My stomach was pumped. My life had been spared. God gave me another chance. He showed me that my life mattered, and your life matters too!

If you find yourself in a similar situation, please get help. It's best to get out of a bad situation before you allow it to take you out. Nothing and nobody are worth your life! You have too much purpose to allow your life to stop because of a bad situation or circumstance. I was blessed to be able to walk away. Life is worth living, not just for your family, but for yourself and God.

Reflection: No matter what's going on in your life LOVE yourself and STOP trying to people please. Don't focus on pleasing men, focus on pleasing GOD! Don't ever lose sight of who you are and what God has said about you.! You were wonderfully made. Psalm 139:14 says, "I will praise thee; for I am fearfully and wonderfully made: marvellous are thy works; and that my soul knoweth right well."

Jacqueline Wilson

Repeat this declaration over yourself:

I AM worthy to live the good life

I AM beautiful

I AM in love with myself

I AM worthy of God's BEST

I AM more than ENOUGH

I AM an overcomer

I AM worthy of the next level life and much more

NOTES

IT'S NEVER TOO LATE

To every thing there is a season, and a time to every purpose under the heaven

Ecclesiastes 3:1

When I first became a widow seven years ago, no one could have ever convinced me that I would have a smile on my face today! It was one of the most difficult times of my life! Can you just imagine for a moment, losing your life partner suddenly and there was absolutely nothing that you could do about it? Standing by my husband's bedside when he took his last breath was indescribable! What was I going to do now? It was two of us and now suddenly just one! Let me tell you that I went through a lot, emotionally and physically. God only knows fully what I have been through! Death is never easy, no matter what the relationships may be (parents, friends, loved ones, etc.). All I can say is but God! He is a Keeper, a Deliverer, and a Comforter. He is my strength, my joy, my hope, my peace, and my everything!!

God is awesome and He is worthy of my praise! He truly has brought me from a mighty long way while on the widowhood journey. Do I still have my moments? Yes, I do. But God quickly reminds me that He has me and I'm going to be alright. I have been so blessed to have the love and support of my late husband's family, my own family and my amazing supportive friends. They have given me the freedom to grieve, the freedom to grow and the freedom to soar! Which brings me to what I am about to say. In embracing my oneness, I have re-discovered my passion for the arts. I am so happy to have been given the opportunity to do what I truly love and that is to perform. Whether it is acting, singing or even creative dancing. All of this is so much a part of me. God keeps on showing me that life after loss can still be beautiful. You know, I can just imagine my late husband smiling down on me and saying, "You go girl, I'm proud of you." No matter what, always remember that it's NEVER TOO LATE and you can make it if you try.

Carole J. Davis

What is the one thing that you always wanted to do but were thought it was too late in life to do?

_____

_____

_____

_____

_____

_____

_____

_____

What are you going to do to make sure that you get started and pursue that dream?

_____

_____

_____

_____

_____

_____

_____

_____

NOTES

LEVELING UP

And be not conformed to this world: but be ye transformed by the renewing of your mind, that ye may prove what is that good, and acceptable, and perfect, will of God.

Romans 12:2

I know you have heard the words "next level" or "level up?" What exactly does it mean? Everyone may have a different definition of leveling up. No matter where you are on your journey, leveling up is to go from one point to a higher point or place while improving your quality of life. I will share an important tip that relates to leveling up. By following this tip, you will be able to eliminate some of the mistakes that I made before I applied it to my life.

Tip: Have a growth mindset. A growth mindset involves living life differently from the average. It involves change. Look around you. Is everyone in your circle positive? Do they have goals? Or are they just living day to day? You should not stay around people or situations that are negative, unhealthy, or at a standstill. You have to put yourself around positive people that are at the level that you desire to be. As an analogy: "You cannot hang out with chickens and expect to soar with the eagles." I'm not saying not to pull people up with you, but you got to get up first. Then as you go, take the ones that want to go. Pray for the others. Your thoughts and ideas need to be bigger than what you imagined. Start right now believing God for all the positive things that you want to manifest. Speak those things as if they are happening for you. Here is an example of something that I did as it related directly to a growth mindset. Daily I thank God and speak "$10,000 comes to me easily and consistently." I purchased $10,000 in fake $100 bills. I did this so I would see and feel what $10,000 in $100's looks like and feels like. I took it a step further and planned out what the money will be used towards. Before the level up/mindset shift, I would have said "that's crazy. I'm not spending my money on no fake money, can't even spend it." I'm not thanking God for something I don't have. The growth came in and I realized if I wanted something, I could have it. So sister, change your mindset so you can manifest the things you want. In this process it won't feel too good because you will have to let go of some things and people as you grow and level up. As you apply this tip to your life, recite the affirmation below each day. For it aligns with having a growth mindset.

Daily Affirmation:
"I can do all things through Christ which strengthen me." Philippians 4:13 KJV

DeShonda Jennings

What have you done this week to meet your goals that required you to change your way of thinking?

_____

_____

_____

_____

_____

_____

_____

_____

_____

If you get stuck, or feel that you cannot move forward, what does God's word say?

_____

_____

_____

_____

_____

_____

_____

_____

_____

NOTES

IT WON'T HAPPEN ALL AT ONCE

The race is not given to the swift or the strong but to he who endures until the end.

Ecclesiastes 9:11

Everything in life is a process. We crawl before we can walk. We walk before we can run. Unfortunately, along the journey of life we have seasons where we feel like we fall more than we take steps forward. Nevertheless, you must be ready for the long haul. The strength in your legs is developed by working a new set of muscles. Each time you stand you become stronger and gain balance and confidence.

Think back to the child you helped learn how to walk. They wouldn't move unless you held their hand. Sometimes in life you are the same way. Fear will creep up and you will have seasons when you need help, but ultimately just like that child, one day you will find the courage to take a step. Then you will get to the point when every time you fall you get back up again.

In finances, business, relationships or whatever part of your life you desire to become more successful, you must embody the process. Accept your current position in life and maintain a spirit of high expectation. Appreciate the knowledge, wisdom and understanding you are gaining along the way. You will increase in clarity and positive energy. No longer complaining or doubting, you will be moved to celebrate just like a toddler who finally took a step and the whole room screams with cheers of joy. Picture them excited and trying to clap with you and how that slight gesture makes them loose balance. They plop on their butt. Yet, for the joy and the cheers they get up and do it again.

That will be you too, but you must endure. You are working toward a greater reward. Envision the end and how it will feel to cross each finish line. The one who endures till the end is the soul that has lived each day like it will be their last. It is a state of consciousness where you refuse to die empty. You live knowing each day you gave all.

Here is your challenge for the journaling space. List your wins. No matter how small. We must learn to serve in excellence. Serving has the positive connotation you enjoy what you are doing. When doing for others with a spirit of resentment that comes from feeling like a slave.

Each accomplishment matters. I pray you run out of room and need to get multiple pieces of paper. Go back as far as you can. List every reward, or personal goal. Write down the insults and stereotypes you overcame. List your degrees, the grades, the people you genuinely loved and helped.

By the end you should realize you are right on track. Continue your journey with the expectation you will receive your just reward.

Auguste Crenshaw

Why did you begin?

_____

_____

_____

_____

_____

_____

_____

_____

How big is the vision? (list all you are working toward)

_____

_____

_____

_____

_____

_____

_____

_____

NOTES

YOU ARE LOOSED

And, behold, there was a woman which had a spirit of infirmity eighteen years, and was bowed together, and could in no wise lift up herself. And when Jesus saw her, he called her to him, and said unto her, Woman, thou art loosed from thine infirmity.

Luke 13:11-12

Have you ever felt stuck in life, where you could not figure out for the life of you which way to go? Have you ever asked the question "why me, Lord?" Have you ever felt so much pressure put upon you that you can barely breathe? Today is the day to get up and make a decision to stand and fight for yourself. It is the day that the Lord has made. We must rejoice and thank God for another day. Another chance to get it right, another chance to try again, and another chance to choose you. Don't stay stuck in stagnation. Someone is waiting for you to walk into your destiny in order to thrust them into theirs.

There are many times when we get hit with bad situations that will impact our lives. Most times it is just to draw us closer to the Lord. It is to draw us closer to prayer and fasting, we must pray in bad times as well as the good times. We must keep our focus on the end goal in order to stay on track.

God has a calling on your life, but you can not walk into your purpose until you decide. Prayer is the starter, but you must also read your Bible, affirm, decree and declare for what you are believing for and stand firm on the word. That is how we fight! Your faith will be tested, but it is up to you to fight for what you want, believe in, and what you know is rightfully yours.

Repeat this prayer of declaration:

Father God, I thank you for saving me and keeping me. In the name of Jesus, I bind up the spirit of fear and inconsistency off of my life. I decree and declare wholeness over my life. I declare that I am loosed, set free, and no longer bound by people, situations, and/or circumstances. I am ready to move forth. I speak life over my life, and into my business. I loose the spirit of joy, peace, love, and happiness right now because it is due to me. Lord, I thank you for what you are doing and about to do concerning me and my business. For you did not give me the Spirit of fear but of a sound mind and I thank you for the peace. It is so in Jesus Mighty Name I pray. Amen.

God is a keeper and in order for Him to fully come into your life you have to invite Him in. Open up your heart and receive Him into your heart daily.

It is time to go to your Next Level in life, relationships, business, and in love. Let's Go!!!

Girl Get Up ...You Are Loosed & No Longer Bound.

Taynia A. Moseley

What does your prayer life look like?

_____

_____

_____

_____

_____

_____

_____

_____

How do you seek God daily?

_____

_____

_____

_____

_____

_____

_____

NOTES

ALL IS WELL

Run now, I pray thee, to meet her, and say unto her, Is it well with thee? is it well with thy husband? is it well with the child? And she answered, It is well:

2 Kings 4:26

When God tells you what is going to happen and shows you what will be – believe it. When He says who you are and who you will become – believe Him. Don't allow any naysayer to sway your thoughts from what God has shown or promised you. He does not lead us to dead ends. He does not build us up to tear us down. So it does not matter what it looks like right now or what people are saying, keep the faith – all is well. They don't know what God has promised and/or shown you. You are not at a dead end.

Looking at our situation or circumstance from the natural eye and hearing with our natural ears what others negatively advise does not solidify our status or outcome. As believers we are to walk by faith and not by sight (II Corinthians 5:7). If it's seen, it's not faith. Faith is not visual, it is not tangible, it is our belief, it is the things in which we hope to come that have not happened yet. Hebrews 11:1 says, "Now faith is the substance of things hoped for, the evidence of things not seen."

Stay the course, regardless to all the negativity brought on by others and the enemy of your soul who is battling you in your own mind. Romans 4:17 reminds us that we should be like Abraham, the father of nations, to call things that be not as though they were. Here is an 85-year old man with no biological children who God promised would be the father of nations and his wife, Sarah, who was ten years his junior. They are going to have children now…at this age? Yes, there are, because God said they would. According to this Romans 4:17 scripture Abraham was not in disbelief and declared his faith. Their son Isaac was born when Abraham was 100 and Sarah was 90. Let this be an example for us to make those declarations. Speak them with confidence, power and authority.

A Shunammite woman was kind to the prophet Elisha in II Kings 4:8-37, she would always offer him bread when he passed through Shunem. As time went on she implored her husband to build a sleeping quarters for him and his servant Gehazi. Given her kindness Elisha asked what he could do for her. She was a woman with everything but children. Elisha told her she would have a son and she did. One day after working in the field with his father the boy died. The Shunammite woman went looking for Elisha and as she was approaching he sent his servant to meet her and ask if it was well with her, her husband and her child. Her response was, "It is well." She was making her declaration. It didn't matter that her son was lying dead on a bed back at home. Her declaration was simple – it is well and it was well. Elisha went to her son and brought him back to life.

Too often we allow what we see and the negativity we hear to be a distraction from our purpose, task or assignment. We allow those things to un-focus our lens. When I was diagnosed with thyroid cancer, I wasn't moved or swayed by the words as they flooded my ear over the telephone. Yes, I learned of my cancer from a phone call. The doctor spoke with a sense of urgency to schedule surgery as soon as possible, but I had no sense of disturbance or urgency. Why should I? When asked, she couldn't offer any information about the stage of my cancer because "it wasn't on my chart". Why was I at peace despite what I was hearing? Because the still small voice of the Lord spoke to me on my way to my CT scan saying, "They are going to find something, but you will be alright." Those eleven words carried me through my CT scan, the biopsy, my diagnosis, a seven-hour surgical procedure (that was only scheduled for two hours), a seven-day hospital stay (that was only supposed to be a couple of days), my I-131 radiation pill along with that seven-day isolation period and through recovery. I'm sure you may likely be thinking, those are a lot of sevens. Yes, they are, and seven equals completion and perfection, both physically and spiritually. I'm sure you have also heard people say seven is God's perfect number. I'm a believer, think of the things He created with seven. There are seven days in a week, seven colors in the rainbow and music revolves around the seven major notes of the C scale.

When we can yield our will to God's will and rest in His promises, life is not easy, but it is easier. St. Matthew 11:28-30 sums it up, "Come unto me, all ye that labour and are heavy laden, and I will give you rest. Take my yoke upon you and learn of me; for I am meek and lowly in heart: and ye shall find rest unto your souls. For my yoke is easy, and my burden is light." Submit your will to His, trust what He says, stand firm, make declarations, get up and move.

If you can identify what or who is distracting you, don't ignore it...address it.

God is a promise keeper. So, don't get distracted by or align yourself with what your eyes may see or your ears may hear. Stay focused and keep the faith – all is well.

Affirmation: I will not be distracted by or align myself with anything that comes against me, my purpose, dreams, tasks and/or assignments. I will stay focused and finish what I have started.
"Where there's life, there's hope."
— J.R.R. Tolkien

Janell Chambers

What are you declaring?

_____

_____

_____

_____

_____

_____

_____

_____

What are who is distracting you?

_____

_____

_____

_____

_____

_____

_____

_____

NOTES

Girl if you fall down, dust yourself off, get back up, and try again.

IT'S NECESSARY

Growth is necessary. Just because you're grown doesn't mean you're growing. Growth is necessary if you want to live your necessary life. How do you apply necessary growth in your life? Growth in your purpose starts with YOU. Growth in your life starts with YOU. It starts with rebuilding your belief system in you. I struggled for many years to grow and walk in my purpose. I didn't have the right tools, or knowledge that I needed to even begin my journey. Because I was determined to grow in the areas I needed I used these three key points:

Key point 1: Renew your faith in God, and renew your mind.
"Do not conform to the pattern of this world, but be transformed by the renewing of your mind…" -Romans 12:2

One of the first things I did when I wanted a different outcome in my life was renew my faith in God. I repented and asked for forgiveness from God, and most importantly I forgave myself, and anyone that hurt me in the past. I begin putting God first in everything I do. Leaning on him for all understanding.

I renewed my thinking, and cleared my mind of anything negative. If you want to reap the benefits of what it feels like to live a negative free life, surround yourself with positive people That are for you, with you, and about you. -Andrea Green.

You can't want a different outcome with a negative mindset, and a bunch of excuses. You will have to let go of patterns that makes no sense to who God has called you to be.

Key Point 2: Set goals and stick to them.

Your goals in your life can be anything from business goals, relationship goals, personal goals, family goals, etc. Writing your goals means you can visually see them. This is important because when you visually see something, it affects how you act. When you write down your dreams and goals you are more likely to be more proactive in accomplishing what you have to do instead of thinking about it. I thought a lot about my dreams and goal, but never wrote them down. Not writing my dreams and goals down led to many years of frustration, confusion, and tiredness. Goals don't become real until they are written. Write your goals and stick to them.

Key Point 3: Be careful who you listen to.

Now, I am not saying listen to everyone. Everyone you speak to about your goals, purpose and your life may not be in your corner. Do have a listening ear to those who you can trust to guide you with knowledge of becoming a better you to make a difference. When you become a great listener you will empathize more, and have more meaningful relationships, and less frustrations in communication. I learned this lesson the hard way.

"The biggest communication problem is we do not listen to understand, we listen to reply." -Stephen R Covey

This quote helped me realize that being a great listener is a necessity in my life.

Easy…..Not quite……Take it day by day, and have patience with yourself and others around you. Continue to listen, read personal development books, pray daily, give yourself a mentality checks when necessary, trust God and yourself always through this whole process. Most importantly understand that growing every day in life is necessary.

Andrea Green

How strong is your belief system in you and your abilities?

_____

_____

_____

_____

_____

_____

_____

_____

What steps must you take to rebuild and restore that foundation?

_____

_____

_____

_____

_____

_____

_____

_____

NOTES

NO ROOM TO COMPARE, COMPETE, OR COMPLAIN

But the plans of the LORD stand firm forever, the purposes of his heart through all generations.

Psalm 33:11

Stop trying to compare yourself to someone else's success! You don't know what they had to go through. You don't know the sacrifices they had to make. You don't know all of the experiences they've had; the losses they've suffered and the entire mindset they had to maintain to keep on going in life. It is perfectly fine for you to see their successes and celebrate them for their accomplishments.

God has placed something deep within you that He created you and only you to do. So, if you have any competition, any comparison within you, begin to compare where you were five years ago, one year ago, one month ago or one week ago to where you are now! Compete with yourself and continue to strive to be the BEST version of yourself. Strive to fulfill YOUR purpose and YOUR destiny.

Always remember that we are given opportunities to start over, start fresh, to get to where we are purposed to be. Take advantage of those opportunities. It's NEVER too late! God has given me opportunities and I have realized that It is never too late. You just have to have a made-up mind and as Nike says, "Just Do It." If I thought it was too late for me to go back into the performing arts, I never would have auditioned and landed the roles to perform in Florida the Broadway musicals, Dream Girls, Annie and The Wiz. I never would have done a dramatic presentation of Dr. Mary McLeod

Bethune at the installation of the Central Florida Section of the National Council of Negro Women. I never would have done other various independent projects including a project with my son, Greg Jr. If I thought it was too late, I wouldn't have started my graphic design business, Graphically Styled. If I thought that it was too late, I would not have started my widow's empowerment group, Emerging Diamonds. You see, all I can say is to God be all the glory!

I have said all of this to encourage each of you that it is NEVER too late to do what is in your heart and what you have been assigned to do. God created you with dreams, so do it. So, remember, it is never too late and the best competition is yourself.

Carole J. Davis

Was there ever a time you compared yourself with someone else's success and felt that your time to accomplish your dreams had passed? If so, how did that make your feel?

_____

_____

_____

_____

_____

_____

_____

_____

What is the one thing that is standing between you and accomplishing your dreams today? What can you do to change this?

_____

_____

_____

_____

_____

_____

_____

_____

NOTES

Girl, You are unstoppable!

ADJUST YOUR FOCUS

This vision is for a future time. It describes the end, and it will be fulfilled. If it seems slow in coming, wait patiently, for it will surely take place. It will not be delayed.

Habakkuk 2:3

Have you ever been traveling, trying to get to a specific destination, the sun is shining, the roads are clear, you are minding your own business, enjoying the music, the scenery, everything appears to be going well and it looks like you will reach your destination on time then all of a sudden boom! You run into bad weather and those once sunny skies are now so cloudy you can't even see what is ahead of you?

I have had this experience many times and the first question I always asked is, "where did this come from? Everything was just fine, but now it is so foggy I can't see a thing!" On one particular day this happened to me while I was driving to work. The fog became so heavy that there was minimal visibility ahead of me. It was the same route I had taken many times. I was familiar with my surroundings, but that day, the fog was so thick that as I looked to my left and my right, I couldn't make out any of my surroundings and it was pretty scary because I didn't know where I was.

I felt myself becoming anxious and could feel my heart beat starting to race. Fear attempted to take the wheel and that is when I did the only thing I could do; I called out to God and asked for guidance, strength and courage to make it through the fog. Then I heard that small still voice speak to me from within and say "Calm down, keep looking ahead and just follow the light because I got you." I sat up straight and that is when I noticed the truck directly in front of me had these red lights that provided just enough light for me to see and stay on the right path and until I was able to get through the fog.

In that moment I thought wow; isn't life just like this? There will be many times on this journey called life that everything will seem fine, but then something happens that is out of our control, and it may slow us down to where our vision may not be clear. When foggy days like this show up and cloud your vision just remember to follow the light! God is our light and has promised to never leave us and will guide us through the fog and darkness that may show up on our journey.

I made it through the fog that day. Although I was late to my destination, I still made it. I was so happy because the sun was shining again that I didn't even care that I was late! On this journey, it is okay to slow down and adjust your focus until your vision becomes clear again. God will always provide light for your path. Remember the sun is shining ahead of you so keep moving forward!

Kijafa James

What are some things that may be clouding your vision?

_____

_____

_____

_____

_____

_____

_____

_____

What ways can you adjust your focus but continue to move forward in your journey?

_____

_____

_____

_____

_____

_____

_____

_____

NOTES

GET SERIOUS

Many are the plans in a person's heart, but it is the LORD's purpose that prevails.

Proverbs 19:21

G rowing up I always understood the mentality of getting an education, finding a J.O.B. (Just Over Broke) and retiring. I saw my parents work hard to take care of our family, but the truth of the matter is, we still lived paycheck to paycheck. We had what we needed, but not always what we wanted. We rarely went on vacation or traveled unless going to a funeral and there was not much left over for extracurricular activities. However, I was happy and have fond memories of my childhood, despite of.

I didn't know much about entrepreneurship at the time, but I do know that I never daydreamed about the corporate rat race. It may have been due to some of the horror stories that I heard so many adults talk about regarding their jobs and how they were overworked and underpaid. Yet, they got up and went to work faithfully every day, as many of us do.

Eventually, I followed in the same path and started building that corporate career I NEVER dreamed of. But God had a plan.

I learned about entrepreneurship and had a couple of side hustles that many would consider hobbies. I was a hard-working wife and mom, so I wasn't very consistent. My job was very demanding, my kid's extracurricular activities and managing a household kept me very busy.

In 2012 my company had gone through several organizational restructures over a short period of time and was going in a direction that I no longer saw myself a part of. I made a good salary, I grew personally and professionally, I had great benefits, I worked from home and I met many of my beautiful friends there.

However, the job fed my family, but it no longer fed my soul. I started dealing with extreme anxiety and depression, weight gain and a host of other health issues. I decided that the ONLY person who could change my situation was me through the grace of God.

I had gotten serious about my side hustles and was making a decent income alongside my J.O.B., so I saw the potential. I had combined my professional skills in project management and consulting along with my personal skill set in website design and social media management and launched a digital marketing agency.

I set some goals that included an exit strategy from my job and continued to work every day bringing my BEST as I had ALWAYS done while building my business on the side in the nooks and cranny of my day. In 2015, I had finally built up enough confidence, clientele, and revenue to leave my corporate job and work in my business full time.

The main struggle I've faced is self-doubt, wondering if I had done the right thing by leaving the comfort of my corporate career, with a regular paycheck and benefits, and wondering if people would actually pay me for my expertise.

But God had a plan for me and He has one for you too!

Quote:
    "A journey of a thousand miles must begin with a single step." ~ Lao Tzu

LaToya Frazier

Do you feel like your dreams have been placed on hold?

_____

_____

_____

_____

_____

_____

_____

_____

What is holding you back from living your dreams?

_____

_____

_____

_____

_____

_____

_____

_____

NOTES

ARE YOU LISTENING?

Death and Life are in the power of the tongue: and they that love it shall eat the fruit thereof.

Proverbs 18:21

I would simply like to offer you the opportunity to see yourself through the eyes of a man who loves you, who worships you as a woman and child of God. From a man's perspective I want you to know that you are worthy of all that you need, want, and desire. Truth be known, it is the true nature of a man to want to serve the women in his life, from his mother to his daughter. He learns how to relate with them by listening to them. My advice to you is to simply make sure that you also listen to yourself.

Listening is an observation skill that requires constant development. It is the most significant communication skill that we have available to us; and unfortunately, it is also the one skill we choose to use the least. Most of our misunderstandings are largely attributed to our inability or unwillingness to listen, and to listen with intent. I need you to know that it is important to me that you know God can hear you. It's safe for you to speak knowing that you will be heard. God is always available to listen to you speak your every thought. I want you to also make sure that you are listening to him and his every word. Sometimes we are so busy talking to him that we fail to stop and take the time to listen to him. I know that God can only serve you best when you create an environment in which you can hear him. More importantly, who and what you were created to be, will form your legacy. When you listen, that legacy will be rich and serve generations to come in a mighty way but that comes with your listening. Are you fully ready to listen and hear God and what he has for you?

As a woman you are the most powerful creative force this world has ever known.   I am aware that both, consciously and subconsciously, you take everything in and birth life into it. I know that you are a vessel that breathes life into all that is poured into you, and when you really listen and hear God you can visualize what he really wants from you. He will build it with you, for you, and for your sons and daughters and for your children's children.   God has assigned you a tremendous responsibility and because of that I ask that you be mindful. I ask that you remember who you are and whose you are. I ask that you remember that there is power in your words and every time you speak you are speaking life or death. As you listen to him you will learn to guard your words like you are guarding your life.

"You have the ability to speak things into existence, and you're talking every single day. Look at your existence. Your existence is what you have spoken. Now to change your existence and manifest the reality you are to live; you must first begin by changing the way you speak."

Baruti Akiiki Abdallah-Nosakhere

How do you know you are hearing God and have you been listening to Him?

_____

_____

_____

_____

_____

_____

_____

What do you think it is about you that allows disguised self-doubt to dominate your movements from day-to-day?

_____

_____

_____

_____

_____

_____

_____

NOTES

RUN YOUR OWN RACE

But let every man prove his own work, and then shall he have rejoicing
in himself alone, and not in another.

Galatians 6:4

Each person should judge his own actions and not compare himself with others. Then he can be proud for what he himself has done.

Ermias Asghedom told us that life is a marathon not a sprint. Competition is healthy. It challenges you and forces you to step up your game. Compete, but don't compare yourself to the next man. If you're focused on someone else's life, you're taking energy from your own.

Each day is an opportunity to be better than you were yesterday. Everyday above ground is a great day, so make the most of it. Look in the mirror and ask yourself are you proud of what you see? Are you proud of yourself internally? Are you happy with the way you look on the outside? If not it's okay, be proud of yourself and your accomplishments. You're not the same person you were a year ago.

In today's society, it's easy to get caught up in what everyone else is doing. Social Media is awesome. It allows you to connect with friends from back in the day. You can use it to make new friends. It can even be used to make money. Most social media users share their life and achievements with their friends or followers.

It's great to see your followers catch blessings and move forward in life. Be happy for them. You don't know their situation. Do you really know how they acquired their blessings? If you do that's fine. Instead of being jealous you could ask them for tips or advice. When you compare yourself to the next person you can create jealous energy. You don't want to evolve into a hater over time. No hateration just elevation!

The next verse says that each person must be responsible for themselves. You're responsible for your actions, your growth, your mental health. Take care of your mind, body, and spirit. If your mind and spirit are strong, the body will follow. Everyone's body is different, but I guarantee you that prayer, meditation, good eating habits, exercise, reading and journaling will improve the quality of your life.

Don't try to incorporate all those things into your routine at once. Start slow, get the first downs and base hits. You will score. Focus on your goals for 30 days. Things will change. It won't happen overnight, but once you step back and see the growth you will be proud.

I'm 27 years old and I feel as if I've been through two midlife crises. I've lost my job, my car, and my home twice. I was down bad, but I won't be defeated. When bad things happen, you have a choice to wallow in your own blood or get up and keep fighting. When everything happened the second time I wanted to quit. A part of me wanted to end it all, but no. That's too easy. Material things can be replaced. Your life can't be replaced, just make sure you're living it to the fullest. Be responsible and take care of your own.

Look in the mirror. That's who's responsible for your joy. Nothing should steal your joy. Yes, bad things happen, but pain is temporary. We choose to hold on and carry those extra burdens. Take that unnecessary weight off your shoulders, and watch life get better.

Quote: God Gave Burdens Also Shoulders- A Yiddish Proverb

Affirmation - I am the best version of myself

Marc Betancourt

What's the difference between competing with someone and comparing yourself to someone?

_____

_____

_____

_____

_____

_____

_____

_____

_____

I listed a few healthy habits. Choose two that you don't normally do and write how you will incorporate them into your routine.

_____

_____

_____

_____

_____

_____

_____

_____

NOTES

Girl, God sees you. Keep going!

TIME IS PASSING

The harvest is past, the summer is ended, and we are not saved.

Jeremiah 8:20

In Jeremiah 8 the Prophet Jeremiah is receiving a message that he's to deliver to the children of Israel because of their senseless rejection of God. The overall message of this chapter is gut wrenching and gives this lamenting prophet another reason to cry out to God on behalf of his people. Verse 20, in this chapter, metaphorically speaks to Israel's state, "The harvest is past, the summer is ended, and we are not saved."

You see the harvest and summer were the times at the end of the growing season when crops were gathered. There were two harvest seasons, (one for barley and one for wheat) and the summer provided them with melons, cucumbers, pomegranates, figs, leeks, herbs, spices, nuts (such as almonds and pistachios), beans, and lentils. After they reaped during the harvest and summer, they stored these items produced from their livelihood to be used as their source of food, and for selling or trading in the off-season or the winter months. There were two months of sowing and two months for late planting…that's a total of four months to prepare for those winter months. The sad metaphorical truth in this verse is that the harvest is past, the summer is ended and they are not saved. These people had all that time to prepare, plant, prune and produce, but have allowed time to expire without making an effort to do anything at all. Time was passing, they saw the seasons changing, and they just sat there.

Sadly, at times we are no better. We should be preparing, but we're distracted and disorganized. We should be planting, but we're discouraged and feel defeated. We know we should be pruning (weeding out and/or cutting off or cutting back things and people that make us less productive and fruitful), but we're too devastated and dependent. So ultimately we're dismantled and disturbed because we aren't producing and reaping anything but disappointment. As long as we just sit there we are doomed. Time is passing.

I have good news and bad news. The good news is, the harvest has not past and the summer has not ended for us yet, because we are still living. That means we can still do something. The bad news is, that we don't have an eternity to get it together. Time is passing. So time out for just sitting there – it's time to get up and move!

Prior to becoming a franchise owner of a printing company, life's hurdles brought unexpected snags and handed me situations that could have left me feeble and debilitated; from the loss of my son, the pains of divorce, my thyroid cancer diagnosis, and other agonizing obstacles and barriers that were out of my control. I will admit I was temporarily distracted and crawling, but I did not stop moving. I felt disorganized and disoriented, but continued on anyway. Although I was devastated at times, and still am, I pressed on through those various levels of what felt like defeat. The late Dr. Martin Luther King, Jr. once said, "If you can't fly then run, if you can't run then walk, if you can't walk then crawl, but whatever you do you have to keep moving forward." Time is passing and it is time out for just sitting there...get up and move!

Declaration: I will no longer just sit as time is passing. I will prepare, plant, prune and produce, regardless to discouragement, devastation and disappointment. THS IS MY SEASON!

"You may delay, but time will not."- Benjamin Franklin

Janell Chambers

Are you maximizing your time?

_____

_____

_____

_____

_____

_____

_____

_____

What can you do to be more productive?

_____

_____

_____

_____

_____

_____

_____

_____

NOTES

Girl, You are the master of your own destiny.

ADJUST YOUR CROWN

But you are the ones chosen by God, chosen for the high calling of priestly work, chosen to be a holy people, God's instruments to do his work and speak out for him, to tell others of the night-and-day difference he made for you—from nothing to something, from rejected to accepted.

1 Peter 2:9-10

Struggles, pain, turmoil, trials, situations, tribulations, chaos, obstacles, and fear will either grow you closer to God in pursuit of your purpose and passion or they will destroy you. Without obstacles we have no spiritual, mental, or physical growth. To be honest, we have no growth at all. Pain pushes us into productivity. It was the pain of being trapped in the belly of the whale that pushed Jonah into productivity. It was the pain of being sick with a blood issue for twelve long years that pushed that woman into productivity. It was the pain of not being able to birth a child that pushed Hannah into productivity. It was the pain of being thrown in a pit left to die by his brothers that pushed Joseph into productivity. It was the pain of being pursued by an angry King who wanted to kill him that pushed David into productivity. It was the pain from the naysayers, the several attempts to stone him to death, and the imprisonment that pushed Jeremiah into productivity.

What pain are you experiencing that you will use to push you into productivity? My fellow Goal Smashers, there are 3 steps you need to take so that you can fully walk in your purpose. Let's adjust our crowns together.

Release your baggage

Emotional and mental baggage will kill you. Emotional baggage is unresolved emotional issues; traumas and stresses from the past (and present) that occupy your mind and even body. Mental baggage is the tendency to meditate, ponder or think negatively about past or current issues that have not been resolved.

What does this baggage look like?
• Unexpressed feelings of hurt
• Unresolved anger about situations where we did not speak up or felt powerless
• Regret about not taking an opportunity, making a mistake or for losing a relationship
• Grief about the loss of someone close or some "thing"
• Insecurities

We have all carried emotional baggage. It is not the baggage that is the problem. When the baggage starts to define who you are, and you don't know who you are without it, it's time to Adjust Your Crown! Goal Smasher, you cannot walk in your purpose and passion with excess weight. God says, "I never promised you a life without hurt." In Jeremiah 29:11, He promised you that "He knows the plans that He has for you. Plans to prosper you and not to harm you. Plans to give you hope and a future." God says, "I never promised you a life without disappointment." In Psalm 34:18, He promised you that He would stay close to the brokenhearted and save those who are crushed in spirit.

Reset your Spirit

Reset means to start over or do differently. Periodically our computers alert us to reset the password, or sometimes you have to do a master reset to your cell phone because the mainframe has a virus, or needs to be emptied because it has become full. Our spirits operate in the same way. Sometimes we are full of our own baggage or garbage that has been dumped from others. You must complete a master reset to your spirit and your mind by fasting, praying, and studying the word of God. You must ask God to reveal to you the areas that you need to get rid of and be cleansed of so you can grow.

Are you ready to adjust your crown? Are you ready to wear it upright and proud? 1 Peter 5: 10(ESV) says, "And after you have suffered a little while, the God of all grace, who has called you to his eternal glory in Christ, will himself restore, confirm, strengthen, and establish you."

Recharge your Energy:

When you have made up in your mind that you are adjusting your crown, you will need energy. Your cellphone, computer, or camera can only operate for so long before the battery needs to be recharged. You must be mentally, physically, spiritually and emotionally ready for the journey. It is hard to fight in a battle when you are drained or deficient in certain areas.

Here are a few things you can do to recharge your energy:
• Rest
• Eat healthy
• Stop clogging the calendar to its capacity
• Unplug from others
• Learn to say no
• Stay connected to the source

Recharging your energy will help you to increase your productivity and feel satisfied with life.

It is time to declare that your crown has already been adjusted:

My crown is adjusted, and I am wearing it well! My crown is adjusted, and I am who God says that I am. I am no longer concerned with who other people think I am. My crown is adjusted, and I am walking boldly and proudly knowing that I am "chosen by God, chosen for the high calling of priestly work, chosen to be a holy people, God's instruments to do His work and speak out for Him, to tell others of the night-and-day difference He made for me—from nothing to something, from rejected to accepted" 1 Peter 2:9 (MSG).

Eboni Montsho

Are you striving to reach self-actualization?

_____

_____

_____

_____

_____

_____

_____

_____

Are you ready to embrace who you were created to be?

_____

_____

_____

_____

_____

_____

_____

NOTES

YOU ARE ENOUGH

Your smile is enough
It is not O.K. to be hurt
It is not what you did
It is not what you didn't do
It is not what you wore
It is not who you are
Because you are enough

When you become the reason for every problem
When it is never them, but always you that is the cause
There is a problem, but it is NOT you
You are only the nearest and the easiest target
For rage blazing inside them
You are the outer manifestation
of the pain, disappointment, dissatisfaction
That eats away at the core
of who that other person wishes they were not

You must understand that you are enough
There is always someone who knows that
And who cares
But you must stay connected to those who truly love you
Reach for them
Seek them out
Forget false pride. Reject your shame
Those are only smoke and mirrors
Love yourself more than you do those who hurt you

You cannot make another person whole
You cannot fix those whose damage
Cuts deeper than the depth of your love
You did not break them

You cannot save them

What is all important is that you can and you must
Want to save yourself

You are enough
With every shimmering sunset
With every brilliant sunrise
Embrace your own wholeness
Let no one talk you out of it
You were whole before them
You will be whole again without them
Do not believe that you cannot make it on your own
Understand that you really are not alone
Have faith that God's spirit will lead you
Reach for safety. Reach for peace
Reach and hold on to the love that you owe yourself
Most of all
You must never forget
YOU are enough.

Gwen Russell Green

NOTES

Girl, You are the light. Now go shine bright!

A FILTER IS REQUIRED

"Finally, brethren, whatsoever things are true, whatsoever things are honest, whatsoever things are just, whatsoever things are pure, whatsoever things are lovely, whatsoever things are of good report; if there be any virtue, and if there be any praise, think on these things."

Philippians 4:8

A filter is a porous device for removing impurities or solid particles from liquid or gas passed through it. If we really think about it, filters are used on and for a lot of things. For example, a lens is used in photography to determine how much light will be allowed into it. Your email has a filter; it is called a spam filter. In social media, like Instagram, there are photo filters that can be used after you take your picture before posting it. Windscreens are sometimes placed on microphones to filter out wind noise and reduce unwanted breath or breathing. When it is said someone has "no filter" that person is known to be direct when speaking. No matter how offensive or politically incorrect they may be. They don't edit their words. They just let them fly where they may and land where they will. As believers this should not be said of us. We should have a filter, and it's called the Word of God. We need to govern ourselves entirely by it.

Labeled with warning signs from the Surgeon General, even the unhealthy cigarette has a filter. Its filter is designed to absorb some of the toxins in cigarette smoke and collect solid particles known as tar.

They are also intended to keep tobacco from entering the smoker's mouth. All in all, filters are something used to separate unwanted materials from wanted materials. Filters are a place where all the garbage is collected. Our cars have filters to keep the oil smooth through miles of burning and use. The air is clean in our homes because we have filters. Some of us have water filters and those of us who do not, we likely purchase bottled water.

In most of these instances, filters are required. In our case, as believers, the Word of God is our life's filter and it is required. It helps us see what needs to be removed from our lives, what we need to separate ourselves from, it shows us what things we should and should not do, how we should and should not respond, it's our guideline to live a life free from garbage and contamination. Begin applying the filter (God's Word) to these areas of your life:

1. What You Think
2. What You See
3. What You Hear
4. What You Say

What You Think – Why are our thoughts so important? Because everything we say, do and even the decisions we make to look at or listen to something start with a thought. If our thoughts are filtered, our actions will be too.

What You See – It is often said "the eye is the window to the soul" and they communicate various emotions. Wide-open eyes communicate fear, while a squint of the eyes communicates anger or disgust. Dreamy eyes are said to communicate love and affection. The real of it is, our eyes are a gateway. These examples are the inward emotions coming out that are usually determined by what is seen. What we look at and/or watch can be detrimental. In His Sermon on the Mount, Christ taught His disciples that the eye is the light of the soul. St. Matthew 6:22-23 – "The light of the body is the eye: if therefore thine eye be single [clear; undivided; without hypocrisy], thy whole body shall be full of light. But if thine eye be evil [wicked; malicious], thy whole body shall be full of darkness. If therefore the light that is in thee be darkness, how great is that darkness!" (AMP) What fills our eyes and ears will fill our hearts. What's in our hearts will become our lives.

What You Hear – You're not gossiping, but you are listening to the gossip. You have just removed the filter and allowed garbage through your ear gate. It is so easy to get caught up and before you know it you are an active participant.

What You Say – "But those things which proceed out of the mouth come forth from the heart; and they defile the man." - St. Matthew 15:18 "A good man out of the good treasure of his heart bringeth forth that which is good; and an evil man out of the evil treasure of his heart bringeth forth that which is evil: for of the abundance of the heart his mouth speaketh." - St. Luke 6:45 Just because we think it, doesn't mean we have to say it. Your thought is a seed. If you kill it at the seed level, it will not grow or it come out of your mouth. The old adage, think before you speak takes us back to the top. I read something once that offers a great filter before we speak. Let's call it the "think" tank. T – Is it true? H – Is it helpful? I – Is it inspiring? N – Is it necessary? K – Is it kind? If your answer to any of these is no, that indicates it should not be said.

Declaration: I will apply the filter to my thoughts, eyes, ears and mouth. I will think on things that are true, honest, just, pure, lovely, and of a good report.

"Think twice before you speak, because your words and influence will plant the seed of either success or failure in the mind of another."
— Napoleon Hill

Janell Chambers

When you look at and filter your lives through the Word of God, what do you see?

_____

_____

_____

_____

_____

Are there contaminates polluting your minds, eyes, ears and/or mouth?

_____

_____

_____

_____

_____

Have you come to accept some things as being okay and not realize how much garbage you are letting into your lives?

_____

_____

_____

_____

_____

NOTES

Girl, You have to trust yourself enough to listen to you and not the noise around you.

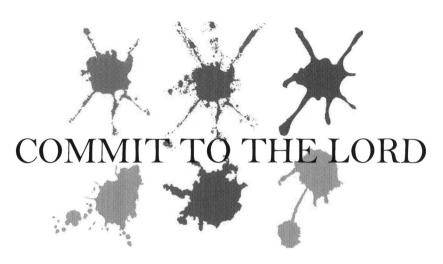

COMMIT TO THE LORD

Commit to the Lord whatever you do, and he will establish your plans.

Proverbs 16:3

You see your destination, but you are having trouble getting there, why? Is it because you are scared of change? Or is it because you are scared to be alone? Some people don't know how to accept change and will always mistreat what is for them. Proverbs chapter 16 verse 3 says "commit to the Lord whatever you do, and he will establish your plans". Without a plan it is easy to procrastinate or focus on the wrong task. Distraction will always be there, but God's plan will act as an anchor to keep you focused. Being anchored in God's plan should give you the courage to make that change to achieve your goals.

If you're going to fit in there's a big chance you won't stand out. Standing out from the crowd is the only way you will achieve your personal goals. Everyone has a different path in life, and it is up to us to figure out the path we are on. Once you figure out your path, you have to make up in your mind that you would do whatever it takes to get there. Losing friends and acquaintance along the path of success is common. Don't freak out, but actually rejoice because this is a way of cutting dead weight. God will put the necessary tools and people in your life to help you achieve your goal. Knowing this reduces the fear of being alone.

No one wants to be alone but sometimes it is necessary for us to be alone in order to hear. Hanging out in crowds, giving into distractions, and chasing someone else's story will not benefit you.

What I think that those things have in common is noise. Noisy crowds, noisy distractions, static of your own thoughts will drain out the voice God is speaking to you in. Being alone will allow you to spend time with your own thoughts and spend time with God. In the silence is where you can hear and understand the plan that God has for you. The next time you are confused on what you should do try to sit in silence and meditate on God's word. There you can hear and accept the changes he has for you.

A new routine can be hard adjustment, anything new will be challenged. This is nature, but it is up to us to acknowledge the change and accept it in order to move forward. Fear of not knowing what is going to happen usually is the reason why people don't take the chance. This is when we have to anchor ourselves in God's word and move in faith. If a lot of us knew the past already, we will look for shortcuts, but to fully live out our purpose we must endure the fire. Without accepting the change, you will never change.

Walking in God's purpose might bring fear to all that needs to change, may cause us to be alone, and not wanting to accepting the change. When you are acting stubborn ask yourself what is holding you back from taking the next step. Submit your plan to God and he will make sure you see it through!

Affirmation - I can. I will.

Joshua Smith

What are you not willing to surrender to be great?

_____

_____

_____

_____

_____

_____

_____

What are you doing today for a better tomorrow?

_____

_____

_____

_____

_____

_____

_____

NOTES

STAND TALL

Have I not commanded you? Be strong and courageous. Do not be afraid; do not be discouraged, for The Lord your God will be with you wherever you go.

Joshua 1:9

As a little girl I was always taller than most. Throughout the years I was often picked on because of my height. Kids bullied me because they were not accustomed to girls being as tall as I was. They were mean because they saw me as being "different" from the other girls. My great aunt, Christola Jones, and grandmother, Inez Robinson, were also very tall women. The difference at the time was they carried their stature with pride and grace. Having role models that loved everything about themselves helped me find my own confidence as I went through that awkward stage of childhood and adolescence.

These strong, beautiful ladies encouraged me and affirmed my worth. They lovingly worked with me to improve my posture. I benefited greatly from the etiquette classes they taught. We even practiced our gait while walking with books on our head. Sitting up straight without slouching at the dinner table was also part of our etiquette ritual. Those gentle reminders to stand up straight, hold my head up high and be proud of who I was made all the difference to me as an impressionable young child. It's important to note those corrections were always done with a smile and loving care.

Grandmother Inez would often look at me and say, "My sweet angel, you are full of grace and greatness because our great Creator made all things in His image. What God sees is greatness in us all." Now, as an adult I stand 6' 1" tall. I am stronger than ever. My head is always held high, even if I am standing alone. I stand with purpose. Over the years I have gained the confidence to know that I am beautiful and I am loved. I was fortunate to have loved ones who lifted me up during the times I felt low. I was truly blessed by the best. Always remember how special we are to God when someone says or does something to hurt your feelings. Hold your head up high and adjust your crown because you are designed and destined for greatness.

Declaration:
My past is not robbing my future I count my blessings, live with gratitude and love with all my heart.

Affirmation
My situation does not change my praise, but my praise can certainly change my situation.

Quote
"Mirror mirror on the wall, I will get up if I fall. Whether I run, walk or crawl, I will set my goals and achieve them all." -Chris Bulter

Bridgette Burks

Are you standing tall during times of adversity?

_____

_____

_____

_____

_____

_____

_____

_____

What qualities do you admire the most about yourself?

_____

_____

_____

_____

_____

_____

_____

_____

NOTES

Making Ways

The door opened a crack
We slipped through
Harriet led us out with grit and cunning
Somehow
We got on the courts
Singed the nets
We got on the tracks
Burned the lanes
We got on the bars and mats
Taught them what they were designed to do
Picked up the shot put
Hurled it in to another atmosphere
We slid into the pool
Pushed the water
'til the medal shined gold
We're told we couldn't
Told we wouldn't
Made the dream glisten with our sweat
Sparkle with our pride
Bore the birthing of new thought
About who we are who we could be
Redefined greatness

With every stroke, every stride, every volley
And Harriet looked
Fannie Lou clapped Sojourner smiled
And we all said, "Ain't I a woman?"

Gwen Russell Green

NOTES

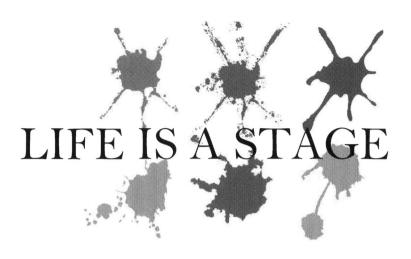

LIFE IS A STAGE

Life is a stage and you have been handed a script (Bible). You have to study your part (Word) and get ready to perform "live" at a moment's notice.

Who is your audience? Your family…your friends…the world.

Every morning the stage is set and the curtains opens. You take a deep breath, close your eyes, trying to remember everything your director (God) told you to do. Now its show time!! You come out on stage…You are in the spotlight…This…is the performance of your life.

Will you do good today? Will you reach your audience with your performance? Or will you forget your lines? Will someone or something distract you? No matter what happens, you've got to keep it moving. The show (life) must go on!!!

But don't worry, this show (life) that you are starring in will be seen for the rest of your life. After every performance, you retire for the night. You go over your performance in your mind and think of what you could do better next time.

The next morning you GET UP, get your directions from the director (God), and get ready to perform again.

Yes, life is a stage!!

Carole J. Davis

Do you feel that it is important how you portray yourself to your family, your friends, your co workers? Why or why not?

_____

_____

_____

_____

_____

_____

_____

Do you feel that it's worth it to keep moving forward after making a mistake? If so, what was the driving force behind your decision and how has that impacted your life?

_____

_____

_____

_____

_____

_____

_____

_____

NOTES

SOWING INTO YOUR NEXT LEVEL

And let us not be weary in well doing: for in due season we shall reap, if we faint not.

Galatians 6:9

Have you ever heard the saying, you reap what you sow? It is a Biblical and natural principle found in Galatians 6:7 which says, "Be not deceived; God is not mocked: for whatsoever a man soweth, that shall he also reap." Sowing and reaping pertain to planting and harvesting and this principle cannot be reversed when it is in motion. In the natural what we sow determines what we will reap. If we sow nothing, we should not expect anything in return.

It is like that old adage; you get what you give. As I have said so many times – if I sow apple seeds, I can't expect anything but apples. There's no need for me to look for oranges or mangoes. Those fruits will not come from apple seeds. The bottom line is if we sow good, we will reap good. If we sow bad, we will reap bad. If we sow evil and discord, we will reap the same. If we sow love, we will reap love. If we sow hate, we will reap hate. If we sow time to ministry, we will reap time for ministry. If we sow our talents, He will help us perfect those talents through others and/or through divine revelation. He'll bless us with more talents so we can share the gifts He bestowed upon us with others.

There are more than sixty verses in the Bible that speak of sowing and reaping. Some of which specifically relate to money and others strictly speak to our words, deeds and actions (which can be positive or negative). It is imperative we are cognizant of what we sow. The simple reality is that "whatsoever" we sow, we will reap. Does whatsoever mean everything? Yes, it is all inclusive. God's natural and spiritual law are in sync.

Assessing and staying in line with the natural principles, let's go a step further. I believe we should not only be aware of what we sow, I am convinced we should also be mindful of when and where we sow. I am of the mindset that, along with our intent, what we sow determines what we will reap and when and where we sow determines how much we will reap.

My natural example is the fact that not all seeds can be planted year-round to reap a particular fruit or vegetable. There are certain seeds that must be sown at certain times of the year in order for them to produce and be fruitful. In the spiritual I believe it is important that we sow when God tells us to sow. Whether it is to speak or be silent, to pray or listen, to hug someone or lay hands on them, to give or give more. I am sure you expected to read or not to give. In all honesty, there are times we may be instructed not to give. God does not want us throwing our pearls to pigs, whether it be our time, talent, or resources. "Give not that which is holy unto the dogs, neither cast ye your pearls before swine, lest they trample them under their feet, and turn again and rend you." -St. Matthew 7:6. We are to be good stewards over all God has entrusted to us.

As for where to sow, we know how that works in the natural. Where we sow determines whether we will reap or not. It all boils down to the soil. Is it fertile? As in the natural we need to be aware of where we are sowing our spiritual seeds and who is planting seeds in our garden. Where is your time, talent and resources being sowed? Are your friends and/or associates interested in helping you grow spiritually? Or are they always gossiping and discouraging you to participate in activities that will enhance your growth? Are you growing spiritually? Are you producing fruit? Are you productive? Better question, are souls coming to Christ because they see the life you live? If you are not growing and are not productive, check your soil.

The size of our seed has no relationship to the size of the plant that develops from it. The seeds of different kinds of plants vary greatly in size. The double coconut tree produces the largest seed, which weighs

135

up to 50 pounds. On the other hand, orchid seeds are so tiny that 800,000 of them weigh no more than an ounce. The giant redwood tree grows from a seed only 1/16" long and these seeds sprout trees that can grow anywhere from 200' - 300' tall with trunks 8' - 12' wide. In viewing this concept from a Biblical perspective let's look at the widow woman who gave two mites in St. Luke 21:1-4. This was all she had and Jesus said she gave more than those who gave from their abundance. The point is that we are to give as we are proportioned. "Every man according as he purposeth in his heart, so let him give; not grudgingly, or of necessity: for God loveth a cheerful giver."
-II Corinthians 9:7

Finally, and equally important is our intent when we sow. That widow woman mentioned in St. Luke 21:1-4 did not give to be seen. She had no ulterior motive and her heart was pure. Sowing is next level. What, when, where and the intent in which we sow is significant. Our words, deeds, actions and giving should be wholesome and pure. "As we have therefore opportunity, let us do good unto all men, especially unto them who are of the household of faith." Galatians 6:10

Affirmation: I will acknowledge God in all my ways so He can direct my paths when it comes to when, where, how and how much I am to sow. I realize I am blessed to be a blessing to someone else and will use my time, talent and resources to do my part for the Kingdom of God.

"Don't judge each day by the harvest you reap but by the seeds that you plant."
- Robert Louis Stevenson

Janell Chambers

Have you sown your time, talent and resources lately? Where are you planting your seeds?

_____

_____

_____

_____

_____

Who is planting seeds in your garden?

_____

_____

_____

_____

How can you give back and be impactful in your community and/or church?

_____

_____

_____

_____

NOTES

Girl get up and go after your dreams. They are possible.

GIRL, GET UP AND MOVE

Don't stop wishing, hoping, and dreaming! Here are some tips to help you to get up and move to help you go to your NEXT LEVEL and live the life God called you to live!

Start - and I mean start now! What are you waiting for?

Put away your fears and phobias - Don't stay stale, stuck, and stagnant. Do it scared! Be bold!

Pen your goals- It's not real until its written. Get it out of your head and on paper. Goals give direction and focus. Where are you going? What do you want?

Grant yourself permission - Just do it. No need to ask anybody when God has already told you to do it.

Do what makes you happy - Live on your terms and make you happy, then you can help others.

Step outside of the norms - Get out of that comfort zone, ain't nothing going on there!

Forgive and let go, because it can keep you stuck - Figure out who you need to forgive and do it so you move forward.

Create a vision for your life and then go for it!

Get and stay inspired. Watch what you're listening to, who you're listening to and who you're around. The wrong people can kill your vibes, your dreams, your joy, your happy and more!

Girl get up and MOVE! Excuses won't change anything...make it HAPPEN!

Rynette Upson-Bush

Meet the Authors

Marc Betancourt is a word nerd that enjoys all forms of communication. He graduated from FAMU with a double major in broadcast journalism and Mass Communications. Marc is a published writer but got bored with it and stepped into entrepreneurship.

On the entrepreneur side he is a professional fitness trainer and photographer. He was born in Orlando, Florida. Marc loves sports. He is also a physical education teacher and works in retail.

Bridgette Burks is an original Georgia peach born and raised in Atlanta, Georgia who works in the medical field and enjoys helping others. Her loving parents, George and Elaine Burks, and her siblings, Brandi and Jacob, have always supported her dreams. Bridgette is the mother of five wonderful children who keep her busy with their activities. Her hobbies include DIY crafts, decorating, baking and gardening. She is also an avid fan of all sports, but basketball is her favorite.

J anell Chambers has an array of knowledge in various aspects of business and spirituality. She is an experienced contract writer and has served as a contract specialist in the United States Air Force, a facilities manager for SunTrust Bank and a product manager for World Duty Free. Her ability to succeed in these positions centered around her love for communicating and writing. Janell enjoys utilizing words to convey precise messages and simultaneously understands its importance. She is a firm believer that inadequate communication can be a deal breaker, but an effective exchange can be productive and profitable. Her writing ability is extensive and includes not only contracts but leases, articles, speeches and sermons.

Janell has a BFA in Graphic Design and is currently a franchise owner of a printing company. She specializes in branding and believes a company without a brand is like a person without a face. Janell is also more than capable of producing publications from cradle to grave given the experience she obtained while working as the editor for a magazine. She aspires to create and distribute a charismatic magazine. Her passion to do this stems from her family's spiritual foundation.

Spirituality has always been a part of her life, as her grandparents founded a church in Orlando, Florida in 1947. This ministry is still functional with multiple locations throughout the state. She is a licensed minister, has a Bachelor of Biblical Studies and is currently working on her Master's Degree in Christian Education.

Aisha Chamorro was born and raised in the Bronx New York, She is a wife and mother of two handsome boys. Throughout life she has always had the unbelievable strength to keep on striving and achieving her goals through her faith, hard work and dedication. As a successful multi-business entrepreneur, she offers more than cosmetics, skincare and cupcakes. Aisha is truly dedicated to changing the lives of others by constantly sharing her Uplifting, Motivating and inspiring views while assuring they can achieve anything. She quotes" God has been so good to me and I want to continue to be a blessing to others, the way he has blessed me". "God is within her. She will not fail." Psalm 45:5

Auguste Crenshaw knows in a world when anyone can label themselves as an entrepreneur that the #1 Unique Identifying Factor is "YOU"! Auguste Crenshaw is a Business Coach who specializes in strategy, mindset, and sales. You can find her somewhere on social media giving a ton of value! She is the epitome of living and breathing unapologetically. Her secret weapon is her Mindset. More importantly, she knows the power is in being "herself"! She loves to transfer knowledge, strategies and infuse confidence in other women in business.

C arole J. Davis developed a passion for the arts as a youth while living in New York City. There she trained and performed in acting, singing and dancing. After moving to Florida, she continued to develop her singing and dancing skills by performing at her church and with high school choirs. She attended Bethune-Cookman University and became a member of the Concert Chorale. She participated in the drama and dance department in order to continue sharpening her skills. In an effort to continue pursuing her passion, she used her gifts not only in her local church, but also at other churches and community events. Always wanting to hone and perfect her craft, she attended acting school. Since then she has done several projects including local commercials, industrials, independent films and the critically acclaimed stage play, Raisin In The Sun, in Orlando, Florida. Over the past three years, she has performed locally in the Broadway musicals, "Dream Girls", "Annie", and "The Wiz, LIVE".

L aToya Frazier is a busy mom of three, who stepped out on faith and left her corporate career after 20+ years to pursue her dream as an entrepreneur. She is a Project Manager and Digital Marketing Consultant. She helps other entrepreneurs and small business owners increase their impact and revenue through coaching and by launching their programs and services online, using corporate strategies.

A ndrea Green is a mother to one beautiful daughter. She has been a 2-year-old preschool teacher for the past 13 1/2 years. For the past two years, she has specialized in creating an infant and toddler, and 2-year-old curriculums. She is currently preparing to write her first potty training book, going back to school, and starting her own preschool.

G wen Russell Green has been a community organizer, freelance writer and poet for more than 35 years. She has published two books of poetry: From the Edges, and Another Beside Adam. For more than 20 years, she hosted the Creative Collaboration in the Southeast. It was an annual event that brought together poets, musicians, dancers and visual artists, to share their artistic gifts. It was based on themes taken from the works of various writers and arts supporters. For several years, she wrote a weekly fitness column, Focus on Fitness, for the Champion newspaper in DeKalb County, GA. She is a chartering member and former president of the Stone Mountain/Lithonia Chapter of Alpha Kappa Alpha Sorority, Incorporated.

Cynthia Jackson is the youngest of 13 siblings and a loving mother of four adult children. She decided to a change careers after being a Certified Nursing Assistant (C.N.A.)/Home Health Aid (H.H.A.) for over twenty years. In October 2017, she enrolled at Columbia College at the age of 51 and obtained her Associates degree in Science (A.S.) in Human Services on April 25, 2020. She is currently pursuing her Bachelor of Arts in Human Services at Columbia College. She believes in Philippians 4:13 which states, "I can do all things through Christ who strengthens me."

K ijafa James is a mother, a writer, and the founder of Let's W.R.A.P. (Women Radiantly Activating Purpose), an online women's support group for trauma survivors. A native of Oakland, CA she grew up witnessing and experiencing traumatic events including violence and sexual abuse began at the early age of five years old. Despite these experiences, she has been able to overcome the effects of trauma by God's grace, a strong will, and a strong support system. Kijafa uses her personal experiences with trauma and healing to help other women by creating a safe judgment-free space for women to share their feelings, experiences, and resources for healing and by sharing her experiences on her blog "Ki's Kindred Thoughts".

D eShonda Monique Jennings is a wife, mother, grandma, and author. She's the youngest daughter of Inell and the late Charlie Hite. She grew up in a small rural town of Kenbridge, VA. In July of 1996, she relocated to the Richmond, VA, area. She has a Bachelor's in Accounting with a Minor in Business Management and a Degree in Early Childhood Development. DeShonda owned and operated a successful Licensed Home daycare in Chesterfield County for over 10 years. She currently serves as an advocate and mentor for children. She is a firm believer of "It Takes a Village" when it comes to our youth. DeShonda also teaches women how to turn their love for children into cash.

T aynia A. Mosley is a Relationship Coach and the author of An Unnecessary Breakdown Within Your Relationship: Communication Is Key, who helps brokenhearted people whether married, engaged, single, or dating become unstuck in their love walk. By helping them to heal and be completely made whole again with forgiveness and love for others. She believes that to start the healing process, you must decide to become whole again, to love, and to forgive yourself, so that you can love and forgive others. It is imperative to love thyself without a doubt.

Before starting Destined With A Purpose, Taynia worked 10 plus years in the customer service arena and now as an author, realtor and life coach. After a successful career in helping people solve everyday issues in life, she wrote a self-help book to help people navigate through relationships and communication matters became her life focus.

Going through a bad marriage/divorce is where her work came into play for herself. Through experience and her faith in God is how she began relationship coaching through helping other broken women become unstuck because she was once stuck herself. Taynia now coaches people on how to show up for themselves in order to show up inside of their relationships. She also offers spiritual meditation sessions where we work on the inner man by self-healing where you learn how to cleanse your mind, body, and spirit through different techniques.

E boni Montsho, is a native of Chicago, Illinois. She is an empowerment speaker, an accountability coach, an international best-selling author, and business success strategist. She has been featured in Rolling Out Magazine and seen on ABC, NBC, CBS, FOX, CW, DIGITAL JOURNAL, and TELEMUNDO. Eboni brings more than 15 years of human resources and leadership experience to every engagement, having worked in corporate, nonprofit, government, and faith-based environments. She uses her master's degrees in Human Resources Management and Business Administration to coach, counsel, and guide her clients to discover personal accountability.

Maudé "Lady Amazon" Nelson is a national recording rap artist who uses her love of musical expression to promote self-empowerment while relating to those from a uniquely rough background. She serves in multiple ministry roles at her home church, New Day Christian Center. Maudé has hosted various events and has graced multiple stages as an actress and a model. Currently, she is completing her first memoir, creating new music, and is continuing her journey of faith in God.

A mber Nicole is the CEO and founder of Justyce by Amber Nicole (J.B.A.N.), founded in 2018. It was formed because Amber saw the broken hearts and turmoil that women were experiencing and made it her personal mission to help young girls and women to see the greatness that God put inside of them in spite of their hardships. Amber built her company to serve God's purpose for her life. Amber has taken her own experiences and utilized them to build a foundation of support and encouragement for others. Visit Amber Nicole's website ambernicolespeaks.com or on social media Justyce By Amber Nicole.

B aruti Akiiki Abdallah-Nosakhere is a certified life and relationship coach with nearly seven years of experience in the field. In addition, Mr. Abdallah-Nosakhere, affectionately known as Coach Baruti is a 10 years Veteran of the United States Air Force with experience in Still and Continuous Photography, Training Systems Management; Research and Development. Before separating from the service in the early 1990s, he also served as 2nd in Command of the Base Corrections and Rehabilitation Facility and as NCOIC of the base Honor Guard and Rifle Drill Team. Coach Baruti is the creator, producer and co-host for one of Central Florida's popular talk show networks, The Brotherhood! MANHOOD! Fatherhood! Conversation Series!, which is providing ground breaking content that is entertaining and more importantly designed to build and strengthen our community, one conversation at a time.

D r. Sonya Poitier is a native of Orlando, FL, and currently resides in the Metro Atlanta area. She is a graduate of Howard University and Georgetown University School of Medicine. She completed her OB/GYN residency at Morehouse School of Medicine. She is passionate about women's wellness issues. Her hobbies include crafting and reading. She also enjoys traveling with her husband and their three wonderful children.

N asonya Rowell is a commercial model with Exposure Model and Talent Agency in Kansas City, MO. She has been featured as a principal talent in Sprint, St. Luke's Hospital and Hard Rock Casino Commercials and graced the cover of KC Brides Wedding Magazine and the Style Section of the Kansas City Star Newspaper. She has a business called The Classy Lady where she uses her platform to encourage women to never give up and not let their past define their destiny. Nasonya loves to mentor and encourage young women to make right choices and rise above the culture's way of living.

Joshua Smith is an advertising and entertainment executive, whose clients range from automotive industry to niche retail. In 2015, he graduated from Florida A&M University with a bachelor science in business administration with a concentration in marketing. Residing in South Florida, Mr. Smith has witness campaigns that have changed the culture. With his knowledge and experience, he is hoping to be the bridge between Florida talent and their mainstream success. His walk with God is short of perfect but he knows consistency will bring prosperity.

Rynette Upson-Bush aka The Purpose Pusher is a powerhouse speaker. She is the founder and CEO of Next Level Lifestyles International, Next Level Chicks Collaborate, and Next Level Lifestyles Travel. Her passion and adoration for helping people have moved her to chase her life's calling to educate, empower, and enlighten people particularly women on how to see more wealth, success, and happiness in life. She believes in everything next level and pushes everyone she works with to the next level of their life in every area.

Besides speaking Rynette is also an author, emcee, certified educator, business coach, and motivation mentor. She has spoken for schools, youth empowerment seminars, church groups, women's conferences, and correctional institutes. She co-authored two fictional books and is the author of the book, *Put Your Mouth On It*, which became a part of the Amazon #1 Best Seller List the day it was launched.

Rynette has brought this amazing group of authors together and compiled this anthology in an effort to inspire, motivate, and move women to get up and live life to the fullest on purpose!

L isaBeth Willis is a multi-talented author and speaker from Ohio who lives her life as a phoenix. Although life has thrown her numerous challenges, by God's grace she is an overcomer. Her first publication, "The Bounce Back: From Heartbreak to Wholeness," is a short memoir in which she documents the price she paid when she stepped away from her passion and purpose. It also documents how she fought to find herself and the steps she took to be restored

In addition, LisaBeth conducts workshops as a platform to jumpstart women on their own journey back to themselves after enduring depression and loss. Her interactive workshop provides a space of support, self-work and most of all, self-love. Although LisaBeth is not a life coach, she believes in life coaches and shares the importance of having a solid support team on the journey of healing.

J acqueline M. Wilson is founder of Eat My Treat LLC and Food Truck named after the same doing events selling gourmet desserts, graduated from Notters School of Pastry Art where she won 2nd place in the cupcake contest for a $1,000 scholarship. Jacqueline also took professional cupcake classes with Executive Chef Vincent Pilon while attending Notters School. Jacqueline was considered as a contestant for Cupcake Wars and she is currently a member of The National Black Chef Association where she was given a medal and certificate for Culinary Excellence. Jacqueline began her career as a baker and pastry decorator while employed at General Motors as the first woman Millwright at the Kalamazoo Plant, where she retired after 32.5 years of service. During her years at General Motors, she was in preparation for her new career by attending many classes and workshops and winning first place for best presentation for Dale Carnegie Class, baking contest at Scott Air Force Base, third place at Life Changers Christian Center.

A Sincere Thank You

Thank you for reading Girl Get Up and Move Anthology. It is my hope that you have been blessed beyond measure and you get up and move and take the world by storm!! You have everything it takes to make it happen!!

If you enjoyed this book please take the time to review the book. Your words make a difference in so many ways.

You can email your reviews to **nextlevelchicks@gmail.com**. If you purchased on Amazon please post your review on Amazon we would appreciate it. We would love to hear from you!

Also make sure you take a picture of yourself with your book and post it on social media. Make sure you tag me.. Rynette Upson-Bush on FB and Rynette Upson on IG.

Lastly if you are an entrepreneur with a great story to share about your entrepreneurial journey we want to hear from you. Please email us and let us know you want to share at **nextlevelchicks@gmail.com**.

Made in the USA
Columbia, SC
12 September 2020